to my grandmother, Eugenia

Dana Popa

not Natasha

Natasha is a nickname given to prostitutes with
Eastern European looks.

Sex-trafficked girls hate it.

Sex-trafficked girls hate it.

OV
DE PRIMAR

tă în via
romisiu
Deviza
sul princ
oastră, veni
mpreună situ

ne, pentru că meri
urnele de vot!

CANDIDAT INDEPENDENT

They ripped a bed sheet into thin pieces and tied my arms up against the frame of the bed. They were all surrounding me, watching the first two of them and shouting. It hurt so much. I could only see their big hands and their eyes. There were so many of them and they did whatever they wanted to me. After a while, I don't know how long, I was not feeling anything anymore.

It was a labourers' campus at the very headquarters of Moscow, I think. There were about twenty or twenty-five of them, young lads; they never got tired of putting me through the most sadistic ordeal. And why not? They had bought me, they could do whatever they wanted, even kill me. But they kept me alive, force-fed me and poured vodka in my mouth. For three full weeks.

I lived in captivity for eight months in different houses around Moscow, packed with girls like me. I was lucky though; one client kidnapped me and took me to the police station in Moscow ...'

    Natalia, 16 years old

'My husband-to-be sold me for $2200.'
    Dalia

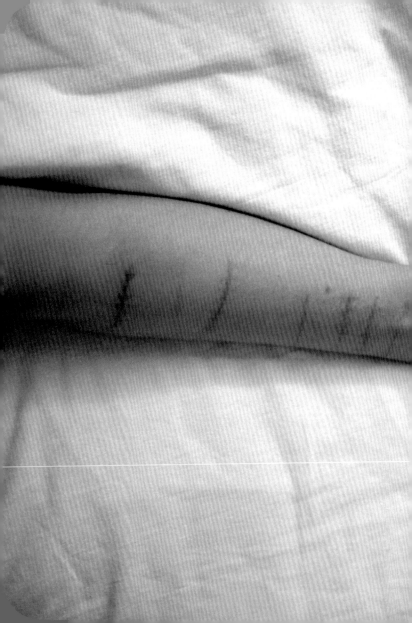

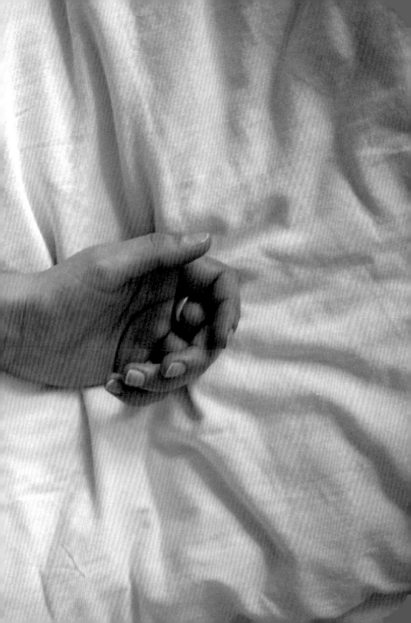

'I was twelve years old. I don't want to talk about it'.
    Alina

'She promised me a red winter jacket for Christmas.
 She promised to come back ... My mother keeps her promises ...'
      Valerica, 5 years old

'... a white car came and took my daughter away. I had never seen her since ... for eight years. We buried her last month.'

'... Don't cry my son, mummy's gonna bring you candies ...'

'I know what happened to my wife.
 She has no fault and nobody can condemn her.'
       Ion

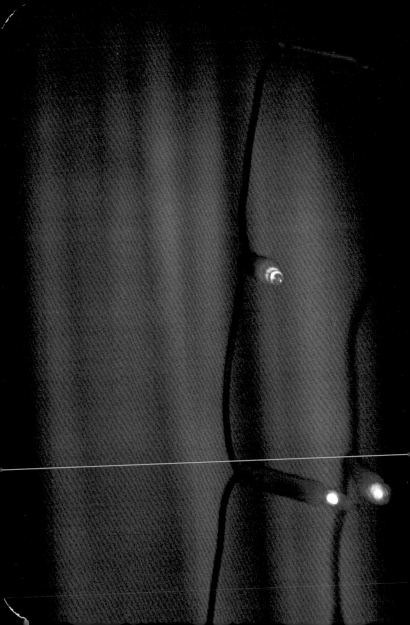

'The pimp tried to induce an abortion by administering pills, but it did not work. So I was carrying a dead foetus in my womb for two months. I was still forced to do three, four clients a day. Only the thought of my baby daughter back home stopped me from taking my own life ...'

    Dalia

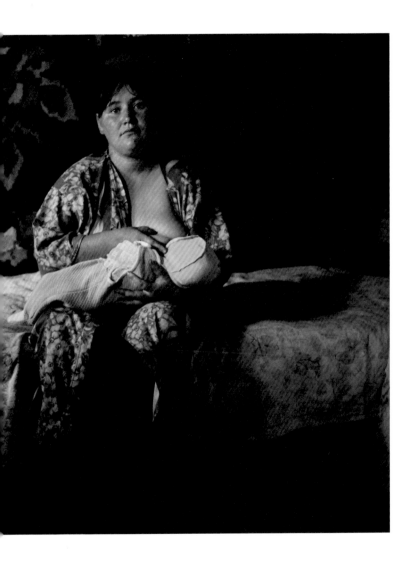

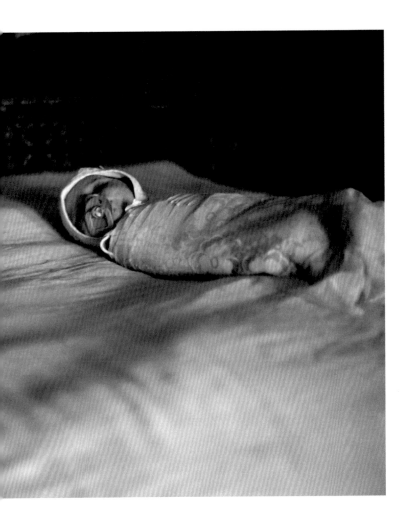

'For one year and four months, from four o'clock
in the morning till late in the afternoon, we worked
like slaves. And never got paid a penny. Terrible
things, that I cannot talk of, happened to my sister...'
    Cristina

'Why do you have to dig up my life again?'
Elena

'In Albania, on the way to Italy, I was sold.
I escaped after three years. I became pregnant by
one of the traffickers and I now have twins. One
of them is sick with tuberculosis. I love them ...'
Larisa

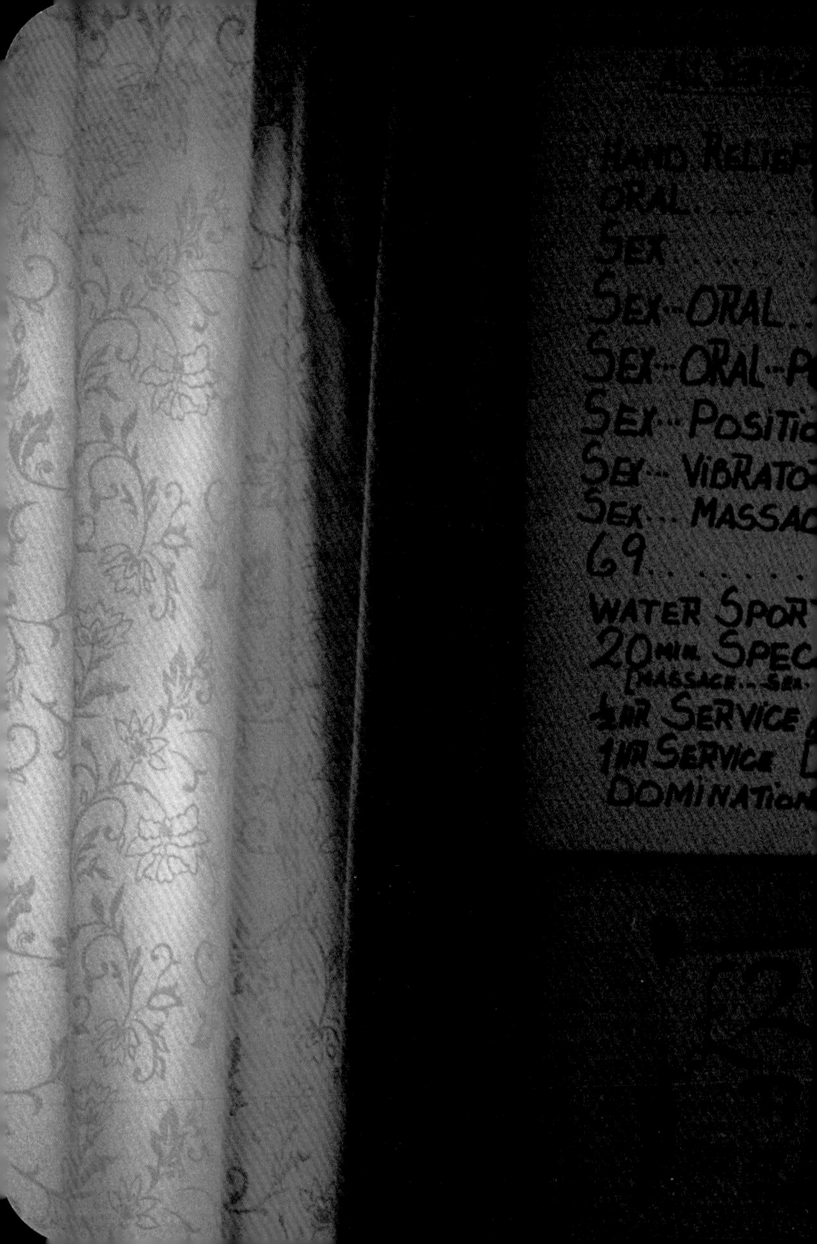

HAND RELIEF

ORAL

SEX

SEX-ORAL

SEX-ORAL-P

SEX-POSITIO

SEX-VIBRATO

SEX-MASSAG

69

WATER SPORT

20 MIN SPEC
[MASSAGE-SEX

½ HR SERVICE

1 HR SERVICE

DOMINATION

A first-floor flat in Kingsland Road, London, seven years ago. She sat on the edge of the bed, her hands quietly folded underneath her thin legs. 'Do you need anything from the shop downstairs?' Mario asked. She stood up, tall as she was, with white pale face. 'Yes, a green apple. I like these green apples.' The red lipstick freshly smeared on her lips. I remember thinking: I sit next to a prostitute, flesh and bones, real.

'That's all?'

'Yes, that's all.'

'I brought her off the road between Onesti and Bacau. With a real visa,' Mario explained later. 'She is better here. She will make more money. She has a place to sleep in.' I knew Mario was his fake Italian name.

Sex trafficking is the most profitable illegal business. It begins with the offer of a well-paid job in a world of dreams. The moment the woman agrees to take the job of a retailer, nanny, bartender or something innocuous like this, the business starts running. She will have all the documents and travelling expenses paid by the traffickers, with the obligation of returning the debt out of her first month's income. I learned about it from the women who had survived sexual slavery and succeeded in returning to their home country.

In the summer of 2006, I went to the Republic of Moldova, the poorest country in Europe, and the main exporter of sex slaves for the whole continent. I went to see how they managed to live with the traumas they had experienced in a world that knows nothing about their suffering; how they lived under a huge shadow of fear that a mother or husband might find out and throw them out in the street. I stepped into a shelter for survivors of sex trafficking. Always holding tight the little fist of her two-year old daughter, Dalia was the first one I met. She introduced me to the rest of the girls living at the shelter. Nadia, Aurelia, Corina, Clarisa, Ana, Cristina … They would all gather in the evenings and share their stories…with appalling details.

Acquaintances, close friends, relatives or boyfriends sell a girl for $200, $500, even $2000, depending on how attractive or financially appealing the girl is. Once arrived in the country of destination, the girls are taken into brothels, their passports confiscated, and immediately put to work as prostitutes. They are supposed to be free after they pay back this debt, but they invariably get sold to another pimp. It's a vicious circle that generates a lot of money. It keeps the business running and the girls in captivity.

Every day they are raped, fisted, bent backwards, pissed on, badly beaten up. They never receive money from the client or the pimp. They are not allowed to contact anybody. Escaping traffickers is not easy. It's not a simple case that one can just jump out of a window and she is free, especially when some of the regular clients are police officers. Being illegal out there can be more dangerous than living in a brothel. Most of the time their visas get renewed even though they are kept in captivity.

I met seventeen women who had been sex trafficked. Some of them too fragile; some very strong, trying to leave behind an unwanted past. I explained the reasons for my work in detail to every woman I photographed. I had to be both discreet and protective. These women were still dealing with strong emotional issues. In respect to their identity, all the names have been changed.

One year later, I stayed at Dalia's place, in a small village in the south of Moldova. The walls of the one-room cottage were cracked. It was too cold at night to sleep. The next morning we took the public transport to Chisinau. Dalia was on her way to Moscow, looking for work.

There are uncountable reported and unreported cases of missing women. I went through the Moldovan villages, to look at the ghostly emptiness of the places where a while ago the missing women used to be a natural presence; the family left behind living in hope that one day they will see their mother, daughter, wife, sister again; kids that cannot even miss their mother as they don't remember how she looks; the woman who buried her daughter after eight years of disappearance; the little altar built around one old picture; the half-empty cup in the deserted house; the bed of a fifteen-year old, gone.

In London I met Svetlana, a young Moldovan who was sex trafficked into the UK. She took me by my hand and pointed at specific windows of Soho flats. In her knowledge, the cracked window was a 'stinky' place; the red light one, a bit trendier. I entered five workrooms, all alive. Many of these rooms hosted sex slaves, brought in daily and obliged to do prostitution. In one hour, I encountered two Romanians. One was wearing tiny white socks and a pink house-robe thrown over the black spandex costume. She was from a city two hours from my native town.

Additional notes

August 2006, Republic of Moldova

p. 21 The red-haired girl. Dalia. Always dragging along a two-year old daughter. She just escaped from sexual slavery in Turkey.

pp. 22–23 Nadia is turning 18. Very fragile. Now she is laughing her head off, next minute she is crying. The psychologist confirms she was sold by her mother in Turkey.

pp. 12–13 Aurelia shouted at me: 'You wanna hear my story? You've heard it! Several times... over and over again...' Ukrainian. 30 years old. Forced prostitution in a bar in the Czech Republic.

pp. 26–27 OK, Clarisa has not shown up at 7 p.m. I am afraid I lost her. Self-harming scars on her arms. She told me she was sold for $800 by her best friend. Fascinating evenings.

pp. 42–43 The girls' confessions about sexual slavery are shocking. Deranging. I am hanging out with Aurelia and Clarisa.

p. 9, pp. 34–35 Liuda takes me to Maria, in Chisinau. 19 years old. Trafficked into Turkey. Abandoned by her husband on the grounds that the baby she gave birth to after she escaped sexual slavery was not his.

pp. 50–51 Visit to Elena with psychologist Ana. Very shy girl. Horrific sexual slavery story in Russia, at 16.

p. 67 The pimp allowed her to wear a wig. She kept it.

pp. 82–83 Elena from Sorroca: obliged to work as a prostitute by her husband's family in Romania. Only recently reunited with one of her children.

pp. 54–55 Dusea and Ana; sex trafficked together into Turkey. Dusea is due in two months. Ana has a newborn baby.

pp. 72–73 Ana's husband knows her story and surrounds her with so much love.

pp. 86–87 I am learning to share long walks in the park with the girls at the shelter. They love the Saturday morning walks to watch the brides of the day.

pp. 58–59 The cottage where two sisters who got tricked into sexual slavery were brought up. One of them is back here with her newborn baby.

p. 46 Gone missing. Mihai recalls his daughter who was once trafficked into Russia, escaped and now she has gone missing again.

pp. 16–17 A notebook; that is all he has got left from her.

November 2007, Republic of Moldova

p. 47 The eyes of Tania. Half-covered by cataract. Staring at me in a state of shock and sudden hope. So much sadness here. Her daughter, Alexeeva Sacha Ivanovna, disappeared seven years ago. People say she was shot dead in Turkey.

p. 41 The deserted house. The unmade bed, filthy old blankets, a half-empty cup on the table and those family photos on the walls. A young woman and her child lived in this space until several months ago when she accepted a job abroad.

pp. 74–75 I visited Valerica, a five-year old, who keeps on asking how many days left until she gets into the orphanage. She reassures me her mum will come back for Christmas as promised.

p. 39 Visit to the family who just buried their daughter. They kept the bag that arrived with Sveta in the coffin. Eight years of silent disappearance in Russia.

pp. 14–15 Today I met Marina. The kindest soul on earth. 14 years old and living in an orphanage. She prays every day for her mother to be still alive.

p. 3 Emotional. Valeria insists on trying on her mum's favourite dress. No one knows anything of her mother. Left for Moscow more than two years ago.

p. 37 Tiraspol, Transdnistria. The bedroom of a 15-year old. Missing for two months. Family makes huge efforts to trace her.

January 2008, London

pp. 6–7, 10–11, 24–25, 28–29, 48–49, 76–77, 88–89 One hour, five workrooms in Soho. They looked exactly how Svetlana described them. The strong memory of the kitchen paper next to the beds.

This book is dedicated to Dalia and all the girls who allowed me to have a glimpse of their souls and dig up a hidden, painful past. I hope I did it in the most delicate way.

Special thanks to Valeria Baker and Carlos Reyes-Manzo who introduced me to photography and connected me to this project, my mother Florenta and my brother Alex for their full support, Paul Lowe for his creative advice, Alastair Thain whose help has been invaluable, Mark Sealy and Emma Boyd at Autograph ABP who made this book possible, Thomas Brandi and Kurt Tong for giving me advice and putting up with me, psychologist Ana Chirsanov in Moldova for understanding my work and making things happen, Iraida Margineanu, Gary Young and all the rest who saw potential in this project. And to my grandma Eugenia for always believing in me.

Dana Popa was born in Romania in 1977.
She completed her MA in Documentary
Photography and Photojournalism at London
College of Communication in 2006. Her work
focuses on contemporary social issues with a
particular emphasis on human rights.

Dana Popa 'not Natasha'
Published by Autograph ABP, London 2009

Published with the support of Arts Council England

Edited by Mark Sealy and Emma Boyd
Designed by Eugenie Dodd Typographics
Printed by Empress Litho Ltd, UK
Thanks to Mark Foxwell at Genesis Imaging and to
David A Bailey, Grete Dalum-Tilds, Indra Khanna,
Renée Mussai, Lois Olmstead, Tom O Mara, Senayt
Samuel at Autograph ABP.

Distributed by Cornerhouse Publications
www.cornerhouse.org/books/

Autograph ABP
Rivington Place
London EC2A 3BA
info@autograph-abp.co.uk
www.autograph-abp.co.uk
Registered charity no. 1127712

A CIP catalogue record for this book is available
from the British Library.

ISBN 978-1-899282-08-1